THE PENGUIN

A Funny Bird

Béatrice Fontanel

Photos by André Fatras

French series editor, Valérie Tracqui

ᴍᴍ Charlesbridge

© 2004 by Charlesbridge Publishing. Translated by Elizabeth Uhlig.

© 2003 by Editions Milan for the revised French version under the title *Le Manchot*
© 1989 by Editions Milan for the first French version under the title *Le Manchot, drôle d'oiseau*
300 rue Léon Joulin, 31101 Toulouse Cedex 9, France
French series editor, Valérie Tracqui

Published by Charlesbridge
85 Main Street
Watertown, MA 02472
(617) 926-0329
www.charlesbridge.com

Library of Congress Cataloging-in-Publication Data
Fontanel, Béatrice.
  [Manchot. English]
  The penguin: a funny bird / Béatrice Fontanel ; photos by André Fatras ; [translated by Elizabeth Uhlig].
    p. cm. — (Animal close-ups)
  Summary: Describes the physical characteristics, behavior, and habitat of penguins, particularly the king penguin.
    ISBN-13: 978-1-57091-628-1; ISBN-10: 1-57091-628-4 (softcover)
  1. Penguins—Juvenile literature. [1. King penguin. 2. Penguins.]
  I. Fatras, André, ill. II. Title. III. Series.
  QL696.S473F65813 2004
  598.47—dc22   2003021569

Printed March 2010 by Jade Productions in Heyuan, Guangdong, Chir
(sc) 10 9 8 7 6 5 4

PHOTO CREDITS

All of the photographs were taken by André Fatras with the exception of:
F. Vidal/BIOS: p. 8, p. 9 (top left and bottom), p. 23 (bottom right).

AT THE SOUTH POLE

Thousands of king penguins stand on the wind- and rain-whipped shores of a chain of small islands in the Antarctic Ocean. They jabber so loudly that their deafening songs can be heard far away. Unable to fly, the penguins waddle around the islands amid the strong odor that their colony, called a rookery, gives off.

How does a bird population like this find food in such a harsh, unfriendly place where only lichens and a few scrubby grasses manage to cling to the ground? The answer is the sea. The icy seawater, rich in mineral salts and plankton, is abundant with schools of fish.

Penguins look funny as they waddle out of the sea. Their bodies are better equipped for swimming in the water than for walking on land.

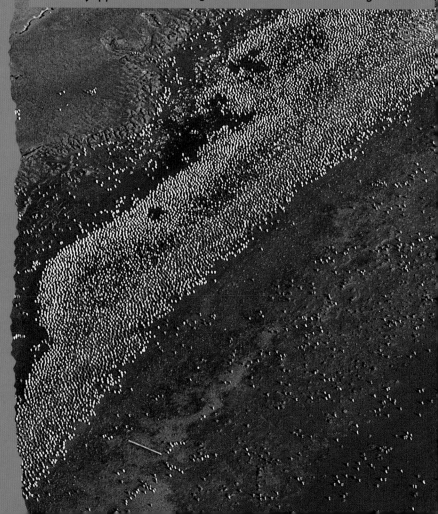

The little white dots that look like snow are actually king penguins. They gather in large groups on land in order to reproduce and molt or shed feathers.

FISHING CHAMPIONS

On the Antarctic islands, there is almost nothing except pebbles and some plants. Luckily the Antarctic Ocean is full of fish for penguins to eat. With their streamlined bodies, short necks, and waterproof feathers, penguins are champion swimmers and divers. Penguins use their flippers to propel themselves forward and press their feet close to their tail to act as a rudder. They move fast in the water, especially when hunting for food. King penguins have been recorded swimming at a speed of over five miles per hour and have been known to dive to 820 feet below the water's surface to catch a fish. Penguins rely on their keen eyesight to find fish, and they catch their prey with their bill.

All penguins are protected from the icy water by a dense covering of feathers that keeps water away from their skin and keeps in air, which provides insulation. Penguins also have a layer of fat that helps keep them warm.

Penguins spend 75 to 80 percent of their lives in the water. When penguins return to the shore to rest, they form a tripod with their tail and feet. This allows penguins to stand for long periods of time without getting tired.

Penguins use their paddlelike flippers to swim through the water.

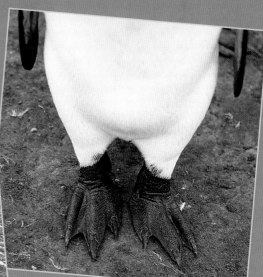

Penguins have webbed feet with claws.

In order to get back on firm ground or onto the ice, penguins hoist themselves up with the help of their flippers. Penguins also grip the ground with the claws on their feet.

LOVE SONGS

Different penguin species have different breeding seasons. For king penguins mating season is in the summer, which starts in November in the Southern Hemisphere. When penguins have had their fill of fish they come out of the ocean and begin their courting rituals.

Male penguins find a nesting area. Sometimes the males will fight over a nesting territory, but once they have secured a place, they let out their love calls to attract female penguins. Each penguin has its own song, which is its vocal signature. This song allows a male and female to find each other, even in a colony of several thousand penguins. A penguin will wait for the other penguins standing nearby to quiet down, then it will begin its own song. Female penguins arrive on the beach and choose their mate, usually selecting the same male from the previous mating season.

Penguins sing to attract mates, but their song is also a kind of personal identification.

Courtship lasts several weeks, starting with the initial greeting and leading up to mating.

Before mating, the male penguin lets out his love call.

A penguin must learn to clearly identify its partner's voice in order to find its partner amid such a large colony of penguins.

NO NEST

By mid-November, the female king penguin has laid her egg. It is the size of a grapefruit. She places the egg on its side on her large feet. Then she crouches down and covers the egg with a large flap of skin called a brood pouch. The brood pouch keeps the egg warm. A few hours after laying the egg, the female king penguin transfers the egg to the male, then goes fishing for two or three weeks. Male and female king penguins share in the task of keeping the egg warm.

This king penguin gently rolls his egg on his feet. The male will keep the egg under his brood pouch for weeks until the female returns.

Each male king penguin claims a small nesting territory. He is ready to defend his space with his sharp beak.

The male king penguin does not eat while he is keeping the egg warm, so he loses weight. When the female returns, the egg is transferred between the two penguins. The male moves his feet and lets the egg slide onto the ground. Then using her beak, the female rolls the egg onto her feet. Now relieved of his part of the job, the male takes his turn at finding food.

The Crozet Islands in the Indian Ocean have been known to have as many as 300,000 nesting king penguin couples.

DANGERS

One of the dangers that penguins face during breeding season is large storms. But penguins are champions of survival in cold weather. They have smooth bodies with a thick layer of fat under their skin and several thicknesses of feathers that overlap to keep them warm. Penguins also tuck their flippers close to their body to conserve heat. In addition, the dark feathers on their backs absorb heat from the sun, providing extra warmth for the penguins.

Sea lions prey on penguins. This penguin protects its egg from a sea lion that is headed back to sea.

Skuas are no match for adult penguins, but they feast on penguin eggs that have been left unattended.

An egg is placed under a brood pouch. This is an area of the skin that is very warm because it has so many blood vessels.

The gestures and songs that come before exchanging the egg allow the penguins to identify each other clearly. Some penguins are impostors and they kidnap chicks and eggs.

Periodically during incubation, a king penguin will rotate the egg on its feet.

Penguins try to establish their colonies in areas that are sheltered, such as a beach that is protected from strong winds. King penguins nest on flat or slightly hilly areas that are free of ice and snow to prepare themselves for the long breeding period in the cold. They must also protect their eggs from predatory birds such as skuas, sheathbills, and giant petrels.

GIANT CHICKS

In mid-January it is time for the king penguins' eggs to hatch. A chick takes about three days to break through the thick shell. Nestled in the warmth of its parent's brood pouch, the chick is protected from the icy ground. One week after it is born, the chick peeks out for the first time into the outside world. The chick is covered with delicate grayish down that gives way to a dark brown coat after three weeks.

King penguins hatch a chick only once every 2 years. They care for their chick for the first 13 months of its life.

A chick is nourished by regurgitated food. This food is rich in protein and fatty substances.

Parents and chicks can recognize each other's calls.

A chick's down feathers are not waterproof, so chicks cannot find food by themselves. They have to wait for their parents, who take turns hunting for food and feeding their chicks. When the adult penguin returns to the colony, it regurgitates a mixture of predigested fish that it has stored in its throat. The chick swallows the mixture. The chicks have to gain weight as soon as possible so they can survive in the harsh climate.

There's nowhere for the chick to hide during a nap. Penguin territory is completely bare. This chick falls asleep in its mother's shadow.

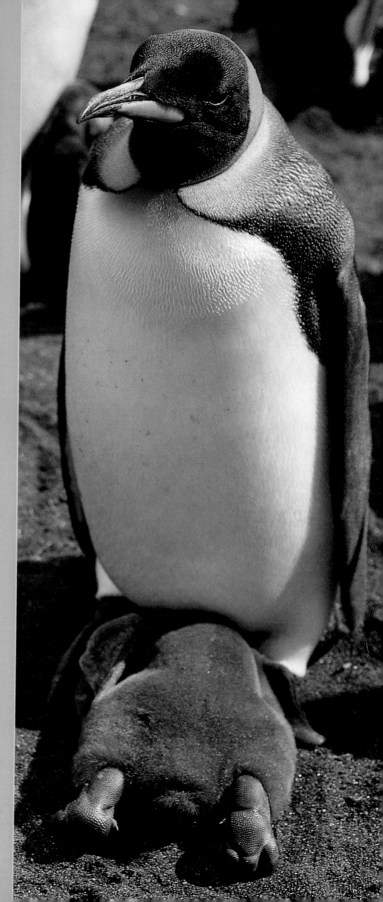

IN THE BROOD

By May chicks that are well nourished by their parents weigh about 26 pounds. But by September, those chicks that have survived weigh only around 13 pounds. What happened? All during the winter young penguins stay in their colony or they gather in groups called crèches. The adults leave to hunt and will not be back for five or six weeks. Left alone in this bleak and terrible place, chicks huddle together with their head tucked into their body, clinging to each other to protect themselves from the cold and from predators. The chicks fast for more than a month and lose a lot of weight.

Scientists are still wondering how penguins manage to survive with nothing to eat in such a cold environment. It is believed that a penguin's enormous reserve of fat helps them through this tough time.

Chicks huddle in groups, called crèches, for protection.

Chicks sometimes imitate their parents, following them around the colony.

HARSH WINTER

Around June the terrible southern winter begins in penguin country. Powerful hailstorms rain down. The sky darkens and the entire landscape looks threatening. Adult penguins return from the sea, braving the strong gusts of wind to feed their young. To keep warm, the penguins and chicks walk close together and form a compact block. In this situation, they lose all aggressiveness. What is important is to stay alive.

Scientists have calculated that by staying together in a group at -22 degrees Fahrenheit, the penguins do not spend more energy than if they were separated from each other at 23 degrees Fahrenheit. These birds even have a special circulatory system that helps keep their flippers and feet warm.

The penguin's body is so well insulated that snowflakes do not melt when they land on the penguin's feathers.

NEW CLOTHES

September finally arrives. The weather is milder. Adult penguins that have not hatched any young come back from the sea and begin to molt. Most adult penguins molt at the end of the breeding season, during which time they fast. King penguin chicks do not molt until they are at least one year old.

Molting is an important process because a penguin's feathers become worn out during the year. Wear causes feathers to lose their waterproofing and insulating capabilities. During molting, new feathers push out the old ones. When the molting process is finally complete, penguins can go back into the water to fish for food so they can regain their strength. For chicks, the end of the first molt means they get to go into the ocean for the first time.

The chick's body molts first. Strong winds help the down to fall off during molting.

A 2-year-old king penguin has a completely black beak. Its markings change from orange to bright yellow.

Since feathers are not completely waterproof during the molt, penguins stay out of the water until all the new feathers are in place. Molting takes about 2 weeks.

In springtime most of the 2-year-old penguins have their new coats. The fast is over and they are on their way to go fishing.

RETURN TO THE COLONY

Most penguin chicks become mature at around three years old, but some don't mature until they are eight years old. At the end of winter, adult penguins return to the same nesting areas as before so that they can reproduce.

Penguins that are not old enough to mate will come ashore to molt. Sometimes these birds start fights with the penguins that are breeding. Other times these lone birds will fight off predators, such as skuas.

Penguins return to the same nesting areas to mate and molt year after year, but they really prefer to be in the ocean. If they survive predators and other threats, penguins can live to be 20 years old.

Adult king penguins have an orange and yellow patch that extends from the teardrop on the side of their head to their chest.

The penguin's plumage, which is molted every year, is waterproof and perfectly neat.

FRIENDLY CREATURES

Formerly the victims of over-hunting, today penguins are protected by international laws. But their fragile colonies, found only on small, rocky islands, are still vulnerable to human interference and ecological disasters.

A scientist captures a king penguin in order to tag its flipper. The tag will allow the penguin to be identified and found again.

TARGETS FOR HUNTERS

During the 19th century, seal hunters killed king penguins and rockhopper penguins by the thousands. They collected penguin blubber to be used as oil. They also gathered great quantities of penguin eggs for food. Nowadays all species of penguins are protected, and it is illegal to gather their eggs.

Penguins are rather curious creatures and do not seem to fear humans. Still, sometimes a disguise is useful when studying penguins so that scientists do not disrupt normal activity.

FASCINATING ANIMALS

It is essential to understand penguins to better protect them. Many scientists brave the harsh environment of the South Pole in order to study the behavior of these peculiar birds. By marking and keeping track of penguins, scientists have discovered that king penguins can swim more than 3,700 miles in three months. Studying penguins also helps researchers to understand the effects of climate variations on marine life.

STILL VICTIMS

The earth's climate can have a considerable influence on penguin populations. There are certain years in which the Galapagos penguins do not reproduce at all, because the El Niño current limits the number of fish in the sea. Even in the Antarctic, where Adélie, emperor, and king penguins live, colonies do not escape the effects of humans. They must deal with disturbances to the environment, pollution, and the tourist industry. Every year more than 6,000 people arrive here and get too close to the colonies. And over 500,000 tourists observe the pygmy penguin colony on Phillip Island, Australia. They bring their vehicles, their trash, and their illnesses. In the ocean, oil spills kill thousands of penguins, despite the constant efforts of rescuers. It is hard to completely protect these fabulous birds.

Argos Beacons

Researchers equip penguins with Argos beacons to track their movements via satellite. Each bird being tracked provides information about animal movement as well as the polar temperature and environment. The beacons are adapted to each species and are designed to resist the strong pressure of the deep sea, where the penguins dive.

All year long in the Crozet Islands, scientists study the immense colony of king penguins.

OTHER PENGUINS

Penguins belong to the Spheniscidae family, which is comprised of 17 species of penguins. They feed on various sea life but nest on land (or on ice, as in the case of the emperor penguin).

EMPEROR PENGUINS

Emperor penguins are the largest of all penguins. They stand more than three feet high and can weigh over 80 pounds. Emperor penguins reproduce on ice fields during the southern winter. The male stays alone, keeping the egg warm on its feet for two months, with nothing to eat, while the female leaves to fish in the ocean.

ROCKHOPPER PENGUINS

Rockhopper penguins have long yellow feathers, called tufts, on top of their head. These penguins measure from one to one and a half feet tall. Rockhoppers put their feet together and jump from rock to rock to get around. They build simple nests in which they lay two eggs.

MACARONI PENGUINS

Macaroni penguins are the most plentiful penguin species. They are slightly taller than rockhoppers but are similar in appearance. Macaroni penguins don't breed until they are around seven years old. They lay two eggs per year, but only one survives.

GENTOO PENGUINS

Gentoo penguins measure about two to two and a half feet tall. They eat both fish and shrimp. Gentoos build their nests amid thick tufts of grass, and the female lays two eggs.

ADÉLIE PENGUINS

Adélie penguins measure about two feet tall and weigh around 11 pounds. They build nests out of pebbles and lay two eggs. Adélies and emperors are the only penguin species

FOR FURTHER READING ON PENGUINS . . .

Gibbons, Gail. *Penguins!* New York: Holiday House, 1999.

Swanson, Diane. *Welcome to the Whole World of Penguins.* New York: Whitecap Books, 2003.

Zoehfeld, Kathleen Weidner. *Penguins.* New York: Scholastic Reference, 2003.

USE THE INTERNET TO FIND OUT MORE ABOUT PENGUINS . . .

Monterey Bay Aquarium: Aquarium Exhibits
—This site features the Penguin Cam, showing black-footed penguins from the Monterey Bay Aquarium's exhibit. The site also offers general information about other penguin species.
http://www.mbayaq.org/efc/efc_fo/fo_peng_exhibit.asp

NATURE: The World of Penguins
—This site offers a history of penguins as well as other information about penguins. It includes a section on the conservation of penguins.
http://www.pbs.org/wnet/nature/penguins/

SeaWorld/Busch Gardens Animal Information Database
—This site is a wonderful resource that covers the life cycle of all 17 species of penguins. Reference information for further reading is also included.
http://www.seaworld.org/infobooks/Penguins/scientific.html

INDEX